Steps to Buying a Home

Written by Eli Berger
Realtor

Cover Images Credit:

© Eli Berger

ISBN-10: 1517754712

ISBN-13: 978-1517754716

*Acknowledgments: I would like to express
my gratitude to Coldwell Banker Legacy and the
Home Detective.*

TABLE OF CONTENTS

Introduction

Steps To Buying a Home is a step by step guide to purchasing a home. Buying a home is the largest monetary transaction that most people will make in their life. Buyer's remorse is common, however you should never sign all the paperwork, walk out with the keys, and feel like you have been bamboozled. This guidebook will tell you everything that is going to happen in the home buying process so that you are not surprised by anything that arises. You will also feel informed and confident as you navigate your way through the transaction. I also made sure to address questions that my clients usually have during this process. In short by the end of this book you will feel empowered.

1

Buying a House is Nothing like Buying a Car

You've decided that you are tired of renting, or perhaps you just received your bonus and you're thinking now you can finally afford a down payment. Whatever the case is, you are now ready to buy a home.

GET PREQUALIFIED: You have probably heard that the first step to buying a home is to get prequalified. Some Realtors will take you to see homes prior to this, but that's not a good idea. Most Realtors will say that this has to be done before you can start looking at homes. This attitude or sentiment is not to discourage you or talk you out of purchasing a home, it is for your protection.

WHY GET PREQUALIFIED: There is a very simple reason why Realtors prefer you be prequalified before they take you home shopping. Think of it this way, when you are looking at homes you are going into someone's home, their property, and they own it. Even if you are looking at brand new construction, where you tour a model home that is designed just for the purpose of home buyers like you to walk-through, you are still making a commitment to start building a brand new home that you will be paying for. Wouldn't it be better to know if you can afford it?

"BUT I BOUGHT A CAR BEFORE": When you go and look at a car for instance, you take it for a drive, drive it as fast as you can, slam on the brakes, and decide you can't go home without it. The car salesmen tells you, "Hey, let's see what you're qualified for." He runs your credit fifty different times and out of fifty - you qualify and get your car and leave.

HOW IS BUYING A HOME DIFFERENT: The difference between that example and buying a home is that a car is much more expendable than a house. A car sale takes a matter of hours, a home sale takes days and sometimes even months. It is a much more expensive transaction and the people trying to sell their home want to be sure that you will not have any last minute money issues that keep you from buying their home before they take it off the market. Your bank and Realtor want that same assurance. I'm sure you want that guarantee as well.

GET PREAPPROVED: That's the long answer as to why you want to make sure that you know how much money the lender is willing to give you before you find your dream home. There is no worse feeling for anyone than to take their family to see "their new house" only to sit across from their bank's mortgage lender and have them say, "Oh you should have come and talked to me first, we can only approve you for half the amount of that home."

A REALTOR CAN HELP YOU FIND A LENDER: When I say, get prequalified before looking at homes I don't mean you can't contact me prior to speaking with a lender. By all means you can come and speak with a Realtor before you speak with a lender. If you know a Realtor and are unsure of what lender to contact, get in touch with your Realtor. Your Realtor will be happy to help you locate a lender because it means you are making the necessary steps forward, in the process of getting your home.

ASK YOUR REALTOR FOR HELP: When you speak with your Realtor tell them "Hey I want to start looking for a home but I'm not sure how much I'm qualified for." Real Estate is a tight-knit group. Realtors work with lenders and mortgage brokers on a regular basis and we can contact lenders for you and set up meetings around your schedule, as well as make sure that you're working with someone that best meets your personality type, and your situation.

Items to Take With You When You Meet With the Lender:

1. W2's
2. 2 most recent paystubs
3. Proof of any other income that you receive on a regular basis (Child support, alimony, royalties)

TYPES OF LENDERS: Some lenders specialize in helping get home buyers preapproved who have had foreclosures, bankruptcies, or divorce ruin their credit in the past. These issues do not mean you cannot get preapproved for a home loan, they only mean that you need to find the right lender who has experience with these very common issues.

FIND TIME TO MEET WITH A LENDER: It is not unusual for lenders to work after 5PM or even on Saturdays. So don't let your work schedule, or your kid's football practice impede you from getting preapproved.

THE DIFFERENCE BETWEEN PREAPPROVED & PREQULIFIED: Prequalification can be done quickly and over the phone and is based on information that you provide the lender. It is the first step to getting preapproved. Preapproval is when you meet with a lender and they actually run your credit and find out what your debt to credit ratio is and then determine how much money they can loan you.

MEETING WITH A LENDER: When you meet with a lender make sure after your meeting that you feel comfortable with this person. You will be speaking with them throughout the home buying process. You want to be sure that you trust them.

Your first meeting with them should be like an interview, where you ask questions about the type of loan they are able to give you, what your rate may be, and if they have worked with people with a credit situation like yours before.

QUESTIONS TO ASK YOUR REALTOR: If you want to purchase a foreclosure, ask them if they are familiar with that process. If you want to buy land and build on it, ask them about construction loans. If you want to buy a fixer upper, ask them if they offer loans that provide remodeling bonuses. Not all lending institutions offer the same kind of loans, this is where your Realtor can help point you in the right direction, but as the borrower, you should also ask the lender when you meet them.

WHAT'S NEXT: Once you've found a lender that you trust and seems like a good fit, you'll get prequalified pretty quickly. It may take a day or two, but as soon as you have that letter, you can now start looking at homes.

When you get preapproved, *Congratulations* your Realtor will love to take you see whatever home you like.

SUMMARY:

You should now know how to get prequalified and the difference between a prequalification and a preapproval. You are also familiarized with how to find and select the lender you are going to work with and things to take with you when you meet with the lender. Most importantly you now understand why it is best to be preapproved before starting the home buying process.

2

You're Preapproved, Time to Search for a Home

Now that you have a preapproval letter
(or a *prequalification* will work, it's just not a
guaranteed loan) you can start searching for homes.
Feel free to look online to get a better idea of what you
want.

As a caveat always check with your Realtor in regards to reputable sites. Not all online Real Estate website are equal. Some websites don't have rights to our Multiple Listing Service (MLS) so you may come across inaccurate information or out of date information with particular properties. The easiest ways to search for homes is to send your Realtor an address that way we can give you the most up-to-date information. If you tell your Realtor it's okay they can also send you listing that meet your search criteria.

WANT'S LIST: This is the time to sit down and figure out what you want. Consider what part of town you want to live in. What school district do you want your children in? How many bedrooms do you require? Do you want an office or a guest room, do you care if they're in the same space? How many bathrooms can you live comfortably in? Would you love an open floor plan? Some people hate the idea of people being able to see their dirty dishes from the living room, so maybe you want a more private floor plan. Do you want a pool? Do you want a garage, or workshop? All of this is up to you and your lifestyle. Make sure you are open and honest with your Realtor. We are here to listen in order to find you your home we aren't just trying to sell you a house, we want to help you find *your* house.

WHEN LOOKING AT HOMES: Once we have the list of what you're looking for we'll go see what's on the market. To start I never take a client to see more than five homes. The reason being, after five homes you become overwhelmed. You begin to mix the homes up, "Was the first house the one with the huge oak tree, or was that the one with the hardwood floors?" If you start asking questions like this then it's time to stop for the day because you could potentially walk into your dream home and not even know it. You're tired.

"HOW MANY HOMES CAN I SEE?": There's no limit to how many houses I, or any other Realtor will take you to go see, we don't get paid hourly. This means that just because we saw five houses on Saturday, doesn't mean we can't go see five more houses on Sunday. Or if you saw a house that you think could be "the one" but your family didn't see it doesn't mean we won't take you *and* your family back to that same house before you make an offer. If you are feeling rushed or ignored, than you aren't working with the right Realtor.

"HOW LONG WILL IT TAKE?: There is no time limit when looking for a home. You may find it after looking at seventeen houses or you may find it after only seeing two. Don't have a time line in mind because I could take you to look at houses on Saturday and we can be Under Contract that same day. Don't be alarmed, Real Estate moves fast.

WHEN TO STOP LOOKING: If you find yourself comparing every other house you see to one particular house your Realtor showed you, you have found your dream house. Stop Looking!

WHEN YOU FIND YOUR DREAM HOME: When you do discover your ideal home, be sure to convey that to your Realtor, that way they can find out if there are any other offers on it. A simple piece of advice, if you do find a house that you love never wait to make an offer because nine times out of ten if you like that house, and more importantly the price of that house, so does someone else and they aren't taking the weekend to think it over, they are having their agent write an offer. You don't want to lose a home that you are both approved for and love because you didn't move fast enough.

SUMMARY:

Creating a list of what you want in a home is a good idea. It allows you to organize your priorities and present these concrete ideas to your Realtor so they can create specialized searches for you. This will also help you spot your dream home, which is the first step to making an offer. Also don't become overwhelmed by looking at too many houses at once, Realtors can take you to see as many homes as you want so don't feel rushed. Lastly, be ready to move fast once you find the home you love.

3

Making An Offer: How much is too little? What fees are involved? What Can I Ask For?

In our market you want to offer the asking price if not very close to it. However ask your Realtor because every market is different. Your Realtor can complete a Comparative Market Analysis (CMA). A CMA looks at similar properties that have sold recently in the area and how much they sold for and can provide you with insight as to if the property you are interested in is priced fairly.

Everyone has heard stories about their friend's uncle that was able to purchase a home $60,000 less than asking price. That is a rare instance and as your Realtor I would love to be able to find you that deal, that would give me bragging rights and a ton of free advertising but that is highly improbable. Tell your Realtor what you want to offer and let them do the research so they can determine if what you're offering is actually going to get you the house.

HOW LOW IS TOO LOW?: If you offer too low the sellers can be offended and in my market they aren't even required to respond with a counteroffer. You can be blacklisted from that house basically. The seller sees your name on an offer and they won't even open it.

Your first offer is like a first impression, you want to show the seller that you like the house and you want to buy it. Period. Don't give them a reason not to take you seriously. Sending an insultingly low offer can foil the entire deal or best case scenario, make things move *a lot* slower.

KEY THINGS TO REMEMBER: You may want the sellers to pay a percentage or possibly all of your closing costs, or perhaps to replace certain appliances, or even to replace the roof. You don't want to offer a ridiculously low price for the home and ask for other concessions. Be reasonable. Sellers often have an emotional attachment to their homes. It's not just an upgraded kitchen, to them, it's their blood, sweat, tears, and part of their retirement fund that remodeled that kitchen so when you are seeing dollar signs they are seeing dollar signs coupled with heavy emotions.

Just like when you made a list for wants and needs for your dream house, do the same when you are working with your Realtor to write up an offer. It's like a scale, think about what you can afford and what you need the seller to pay. Every state has different fees, some may see it as a price for a lender while other states may see it as buyer fee. Be sure to check with your Realtor in your area.

HOME WARRANTIES: You may ask the seller's to pay for a Home Warranty. This will cover any appliances or issues with the house for a year after you move in. This way you don't have to file an insurance claim or pay out of pocket for repairs. This is a great option if you are purchasing an older home. Be sure to ask your realtor about this option, even if you have to pay for some or all of it, it is something that has saved my clients lots of money in the long run.

SIGNING THE OFFER: When you've settled on an offer price you will then be asked to sign the offer. It's a sixteen page document. Depending on the house there may be more documents. After you sign and leave our office we call the other agent to inform them that we're going to be sending them an offer. As long as they don't respond with, "We just went under agreement," we will then scan and email your offer to them.

WHAT'S INCLUDED IN THE OFFER: Your offer will include your prequalification letter however as your Realtor I will contact your lender and ask them for an updated letter that reflects the price you are offering to purchase the home. For instance if you are prequalified for $220,000 but you find a house that is $175,000 and you are offering $170,000 we will have your lender send us an updated prequalification letter that states you are preapproved for $170,000. That way you are showing the seller that you can afford what you are offering to pay, however it doesn't let them see your cards.

It's like playing poker, you would never show the other players at the table what you've got. A new offer letter will be generated every time you and the seller negotiate on the price.

A BRIEF WORD ON COUNTEROFFERS: Once you submit your offer to the sellers they may counter. They may counter on the price or they may counter on the closing date, they have the right to counter on any of the concession you requested like, closing costs. When they counter, it does not mean you have to accept. You can counter their counter. And this will go on until you agree on the terms of sale.

THINGS TO REMEMBER WHEN COUNTERING: If you love the house do not offend your seller by submitted multiple counter offers where you are arguing over $1-$2 thousand dollars. At this point you are nickel and diming and the seller may just walk away from the deal. I'm not a lender but there is a rule of thumb, for every thousand it's approximately $8-10 differences on your monthly payments. So if you really want the house don't risk losing it over $10 a month or $3,600 over 30 years.

SUMMARY:

When you find the house that you want you decide upon a price and make an offer to purchase. This sixteen page document is written to protect all parties involved. Remember when determining how much you want to offer to enlist the expertise of your Realtor along with what concessions you may ask the seller for. This is your first interaction with the sellers, so be sure to make it the right one.

4

Earnest Money: What is It? How Much is It? Can I Get It Back?

We've all heard *the term Earnest money.*
Unless you've previously purchased a home you may
not know what it is. Earnest money is not a down
payment. Earnest money is good faith money, it is the
glue that holds the contract together. Once the deal is
accepted then you are responsible for providing the

earnest money. You can give it to your Realtor who will promptly turn it over to the title company or you can give it to the title company yourself. (This will depend on what state you're in, ask your Realtor what your state's laws dictate).

HOW MUCH IS EARNEST MONEY: The smallest amount of earnest money I've seen is $500, which is also quite common in New Mexico, and the largest I've seen is $10,000. This amount is predetermined in your offer so it will not sneak up on you. You will write the check out to the Title Company or Escrow Company. It gets deposited into an account with the title company. It is a very controlled trust account which isn't taxed. Your check will be cashed however, and once we close that will be used as part of your down payment or if there's extra then it is returned to you. That money does not go to anyone else, it remains yours.

What everyone asks when they bring in this check is, "If the deal goes sour for any reason, breach of contract, lending fell through, etc. will I get this money back?" and the answer is YES. This is also written within the offer.

KEY THINGS TO REMEMBER WHEN UNDER AGREEMENT: The biggest mistake a buyer can do while under contract is to run up there credit. Do not buy anything on credit until after you close. The lender will check your credit score one more time before closing and any big purchases can affect your score, causing you to lose your house.

I've had clients buy brand new furniture for their brand new house only to lose their home loan and not move in because they bought it all on credit cards. I even had another client buy an airplane, yes they took out a loan to purchase a plane, and the bank denied their home loan because of it.

A preapproval states that the lender will loan you the money for your home as long as your debt to credit ratio does not change. When you make large purchases your debt ratio goes up causing your credit ratio to go down. The banks don't like this, it makes them nervous and can cost you your home.

If there is an emergency and you have to charge something, ask your lender first.

"WHEN WON'T I GET MY EARNEST MONEY BACK?":
It is also written within the offer the circumstances in which you will not have your earnest money returned to you. For instance, if your financing falls through and you fail to notify anyone you may lose your earnest money, even though losing your financing is usually a reason when you would receive your earnest money back.

Basically be up front with any changes that occur to you financially that may upset the deal. Of course if you do not follow the deadlines written within the contract, or you simply 'change your mind' these are both circumstances where you may not receive your earnest money back.

SUMMARY:

Earnest money is the glue that holds the transaction together. The amount of earnest money is predetermined and written within the original offer along with the terms of which you will receive it back if the deal falls through. Be careful not to purchase anything on credit while you are Under Agreement. Anything that will cause your debt to credit ratio to change can cause you to lose your home loan rendering you incapable of closing.

5

Avoid Surprises: What a Home Inspection Can Tell You

Once you're under agreement on your home, the next step is to order a home inspection. There is a section on the offer that allows you to waive inspections, however unless you have a very good reason for doing so, I am going to say, "For your protection, get a home inspection."

COST OF A HOME INSPECTION: Home inspections can range in price. In our market it is usually around $200. You can ask the sellers to pay for a part of the inspection, but usually it is something the buyer will pay for. Most of the home inspectors in our market do give buyer's the option to pay for the inspection at the time of closing rather than at the time of service. As a buyer you are always invited to go to the home inspection so you can see what the inspector is seeing. That way you have less questions when you receive the inspection report. *I am a Realtor, in order to provide you with the most accurate information, I interviewed local home inspector Carlos Hill, who owns and operates his own home inspection company, The Home Detective.

CHOOSING A HOME INSPECTER: Home inspectors all look at the structure, the roof, heating and cooling systems, the electrical systems and plumbing. Really everything they can look at without taking it apart. Their goals is to provide a comprehensive overview of the home. Certain home inspectors may look at appliances, like washers and dryers, refrigerators, landscaping systems, even irrigation systems. Those can take days in order to be conducted properly. If you want those things reviewed make sure you choose an inspector that includes those things in their report.

Lastly, when choosing an Inspector, your Realtor cannot choose one for you. That choice has to be made by you. We can provide you with a list of who we have worked with to help you decide.

WHAT DO HOME INSPECTORS LOOK FOR: Home inspectors look for indicators that are situation specific. For example with a roof, they look for changes in the overall structure. When they climb up on the roof and see a large bow they may hire a structural engineer to determine if any portion of the roof is in fact failing. If something is failing, that means it needs to be replaced.

FIRE DAMAGE: In the case of fire damage, a home inspector will not only look at the place where the incident occurred but also check for smoke damage in the attic, and other places that the homeowner may have missed when they repaired the damage from the fire.

MOLD: A home inspector does not need to complete a separate mold report however they will look for conducive conditions that would let mold grow. If mold is found they can test to identify the type of mold which will tell them how to treat it and how to address the issue. It's very easy to treat.

TERMITES: In our state a termite report is a separate report. Termites that are in the United States vary by area. In New Mexico we have different termites than California or Louisiana. Termites in New Mexico will live in a colony outside and then enter the home in order to eat after which they will return to their colony. In Louisiana or California they will eat the inside of the house and live there. Inside of a house termites love to eat drywall, so inspectors look for damage to the sheet rock, because it is solid indicator that termites are present.

NMPA 33 FORM: In New Mexico termite certified inspectors need to complete this form which states the house is clear of termites or not. Lenders will require this.

"DO I NEED TO FIX EVERYTHING ON THE INSPECTION REPORT?": A home inspection will tell you anything and everything that is wrong with the house, and anything and everything that will go wrong with the house. Do not let the home inspection scare you, in fact look at it as a great resource. Now you know exactly what you're getting into. Not everything that the home inspector shows you needs to be repaired or replaced right away. It is their job to tell you, from their experience, what they may foresee happening.

DISCLAIMER: Home inspections are for information only, so that you know what you are buying.

SUMMARY:

A home inspection can reveal pre-existing problems with as well as issues that may arise after you move in. After the inspection report is delivered to both yourself and the sellers, negotiations in terms of the cost of repairs will commence. Inspection reports are for information purposes only and should not serve

as cause for alarm.

6

WOR's: Your Dream Home Is in Need of Repairs: What Are Your Options?

Once you have the inspection report a copy of it gets sent to the listing agent. At this time you sit down with your Realtor and discuss what repairs you want done prior to occupying the house, and who you want to pay for them. This document is called, **Objections, Waivers, and Resolutions** or WOR's. This is all negotiable.

ASKING THE SELLER TO PAY FOR REPAIRS: Keep in mind this is when, if you lowballed the offer, your sellers may not be willing to put money into the cost of repairs. However it is also the time where you can walk away from the deal and still get your earnest money. If the inspection report revealed far too many issues then it is your prerogative to walk away.

SHOULD YOU STAY OR SHOULD YOU GO?: All properties are going to have an inspection report that requires some repairs so don't let the presence of repairs frighten you away. You aren't buying a "money pit" just because the house needs a new roof. In fact there are many ways to get a new roof on the home prior to closing, perhaps you have the sellers pay for it and you pick the roofer, or maybe you pay for half and the sellers pay for half and you produce your half at closing rather than upfront prior to the work being done. Or maybe you pay for half and have the sellers raise the price of the home to cover your end. When it comes to repairs or even appliances needing to be replaced, it is all negotiable.

SUMMARY:

Once you have decided upon what repairs are going to commence and who is paying for it and how, then you should feel at ease because you are getting closer to moving into your new home. Remember if you cannot reach an agreement you can still back out of the deal and receive your earnest money back, however every house will need some sort of repairs.

7

Ordering an Appraisal: What's The Difference Between an Appraisal and an Inspection?

Now that you have the inspection and you know what you are buying then your Realtor calls the lender to order the appraisal. You cannot choose your appraiser. This is someone that the bank hires and in the state of New Mexico it is completely randomized so that even the bank does not know who the appraiser will be.

PURPOSE OF A HOME APPRAISAL: Once the home appraises, which means the appraiser went out and looked at the market value of the home, and utilized their system in order to find out how much the house is worth. If the amount of the home appraises for less than what you are purchasing it for there is a problem. The lender will only finance the appraised value. If this is the case then we have to re-enter negotiations to either lower the price of the home or figure out who is going to pay the difference between the appraised value and the accepted offer price. This can also terminate the deal and we will have to find another home. This is not like an inspection where you can make repairs to the home to change the value.

WHAT'S NEXT: If it appraises at market value then we move forward. Now we enter the waiting game. We wait for the repairs to be completed and for the title company to complete their work.

HOME INSURANCE: As a buyer, you should be working on getting home insurance because you will need that prior to closing.

SUMMARY:

When your bank orders the appraisal two things can happen. The home can either appraise, meaning it is worth the same amount or more than the accepted sales price or it is worth less. When it is worth less than the sales price, negotiations are reopened. At the time of the appraisal buyers should begin looking for home insurance since it is requirement by lenders to have it prior to closing on the house.

8

Paperwork You Will Be Presented With Prior To Closing: Survey, Covenants, Liens on Title or Buyer, Property Disclosure

Oftentimes buyers feel like they aren't having to do anything, why can't we close after the appraisal?

In fact there is a great amount of things being done, "behind the scenes." The tile company is making sure that the title is clear on the home. They are making sure the buyer and seller do not have any liens. Any court liens will need to be settled before you purchase the property. The title company is also entrusted with providing us with paperwork to look over prior to closing.

SURVEY: The first document that must be evaluated is the survey. The survey will show you where your property line is. It will reveal if your neighbor's fence is indeed on their property or if it infringes upon yours. More importantly the survey will show if the house you looked at, fell in love with, and just had an inspection done on, is the same house that the county has recorded. The survey will tell you all of this. In New Mexico we try and provide you with the survey prior to even making an offer, because we don't want any surprises, like finding out the guest house that you were planning on moving your mother-in-law into isn't even built on your property.

RESTRICTIVE COVENANTS: The next document that accompanies many residential real estate transactions are the Covenants. Restrictive covenants will tell you what you can and can't do to your home. For instance if you are buying a home in a gated community there will be a plethora of things that the Homeowners Association has deemed as unacceptable to do to your home. Even in neighborhoods without a gate there may be restrictions to how tall your fence can be, or where you can mount solar panels. All of this should be read over prior to closing so again, you know what you're buying.

PROPERTY DISCLOSURE: The property disclosure is something we try and make available to you prior to making the offer in New Mexico. A property disclosure is to be completed by the seller. Their Realtor cannot help them with it. This tells you any and everything about the property from the seller's perspective. This is helpful because they have owned the home and in some cases actually lived in it so they can tell you about the house's quirks. The information provided on the property disclosure should be consistent with the inspection report. However if something appears on the inspection report that wasn't on the property disclosure, do not immediately blame the seller. The inspector has more knowledge about what a home should look like. Which is why you should never waive your right to an inspection in lieu of a property disclosure.

GENERAL WARRANTY DEED: This is not a document you will receive prior to closing but it perhaps the most important document that will show who owns the property after closing. A general warranty deed is the most commonly used deed in a residential real estate transaction. With this deed there are no liens so after closing the deed can be recorded in your name and the property is now yours.

SUMMARY:

Important documents to look over before you close on your new home include the survey. The survey shows you exactly what property you are acquiring with this sale. Second is the Restrictive Covenants, which express the rules and conditions associated with your particular property. Third is the property disclosure which states a detailed account of the home based on the knowledge of the seller. Lastly is the General Warranty Deed, which you will not receive until closing, but is the legal document that states who owns the house.

9

Final Walk-Thru

A final walk-thru is the final step you will take before you close on your new home. You and your Realtor will set up a time, the week before your closing date to 'walk' the property.

At this time you want to look for any changes made to the property. You want to make sure that everything in the house is in the same condition it was in prior to making the offer.

Obviously the repairs that were agreed upon should already be completed as well. As long as nothing has been changed in the home, and the repairs are completed you can sign the **Final-Walk Thru Form** and closing can proceed as scheduled.

If for some reason the home is not the in same condition that is was when you offered to purchase the property than closing may be delayed or at the worst, cancelled.

WHAT TO LOOK FOR: During the final walk-thru, you are looking for intentional changes to the property. For instance, different cabinets, stripped paint, missing flooring. Major changes like, the windows have been replaced with cheaper single paned windows but when you first saw the home, and when you wrote the offer, you were under the impression that you would be buying a home with double panned windows.

Dust or just regular symptoms of a vacant home are not things that you should concern yourself with when conducting the final walk-thru, you are looking for major changes. Also if you negotiate that new appliances were going to be placed in the home, during the walk thru you should see those appliances.

SUMMARY:

The final-walk thru allows you to look for any massive changes to the house before you close. It is scheduled about a week before closing and is done with your Realtor. If any changes or modifications have been made to the property you may have to postpone or cancel closing. The final walk-thru is also the time when you would check to make sure that all the agreed upon repairs have been made.

10

Closing Procedures

Prior to closing, you, your realtor, the listing agent, sellers, and the title company will receive what is called the HUD-1 Settlement Document from the lender. The HUD states where every penny goes that is contributed to the sale. For instance closing costs, repairs, home warranties. It's like a receipt of your purchase. If everyone approves of the HUD then the lender goes through final underwriting, and finally we are sitting at the closing table.

"WHO IS AT CLOSING?": Closing is very intimate. It includes your real estate agent, the closing officer and the party selling and you, the buyers. Actually in New Mexico, the party selling the home, is not present it's just the buyers. The sellers have their own separate closing. During closing the closing officer will walk you through every document that you sign. Some of the documents you are asked to sign, you have already seen, they are copies of the documents that were discussed in chapter eight. They will also go over your rate, your lending process, your monthly payment, etc. At this time you will sign the deed, the mortgage lien, and a document explaining what happens if you fail to pay your mortgage. While you are signing the documents are being notarized by the closing officer. The reason everything is being notarized is to confirm that the person buying the property is actually you.

WHAT TO TAKE TO CLOSING: Make sure you take two forms of identification along with a cashier check for your closing costs.

REMEMBER TO TURN ON THE UTILITIES: After you sign you want to make sure you turn on the utilities. You want to do that as fast as you can, because some sellers may have the utilities turned off.

"WHEN DO I GET THE KEYS?": You signed all your paperwork now you're walking away, we don't just give you the keys. It as to be **recorded and funded**. Once you sign all the documents, the closing agent gathers all the documents, and send them back to the lender to review it. The lender will then process them, this can take up to an hour or two. After this is completed the lender will send the wire authorization code to the title company, allowing them to move forward with funding the deal. Once the deal is funded and it is recorded in the county as a purchase of the home that's when you get a call from your Realtor stating that it has been recorded and funded and you get your keys. Once you have the keys you can move in!

IT'S NOT GOODBYE: Most realtors are always accessible to you. Just because we've closed on the house doesn't mean you can never contact them again, and I'm not just referring to selling your homed down the line. If an issue comes up after you have keys you can always call your Realtor. You are always their client.

SUMMARY:

Closing is a small intimate process where everything that you sign is explained to you one-on-one by the closing agent. Remember to take a cashier's check to pay your portion of the closing costs along with two forms of valid identification. All fees associated with the purchase of your home are stated on the HUD-1 Settlement Statement prior to closing. You will receive keys after the deal has been both recorded and funded. Always feel free to contact your Realtor even after the deal is closed. They are there to help.

About the Author

Eli Berger is a Realtor with Coldwell Banker Legacy in Las Cruces, New Mexico. He specializes in both Residential and Commercial Real Estate Transactions. He prides himself on providing his clients with exemplary service

by educating his clients as they navigate through the buying or selling process. If you have any questions don't hesitate to contact Eli at, Elibergerrealtor.com or (575) 528-8615

Cell: (575) 528-8615
Office: (575) 521-1000
Eli@bergerrealtor.com

LOOK OUT FOR ELI'S NEXT BOOK

Steps to Listing a Home